Contents

Spring Has Come!

■ **Listen to the story.** ■ **Listen and circle.**

T1

Winter is finally over.
Everything is turning green!

1

Frog**s** are singing in the lake.

frog

2

They **h**o**p** from plant to plant.

③

hop

A bear **cub** is **ru**bbing his nose on his mom.

④

cub

Mom gives him a big **hug** and a thousand kisses.

hug

⑤

There is a big **clock** tower.

clock

⑥

You can see green **moss** on the tower.

moss

Spring has come!

T2

A Listen and repeat.

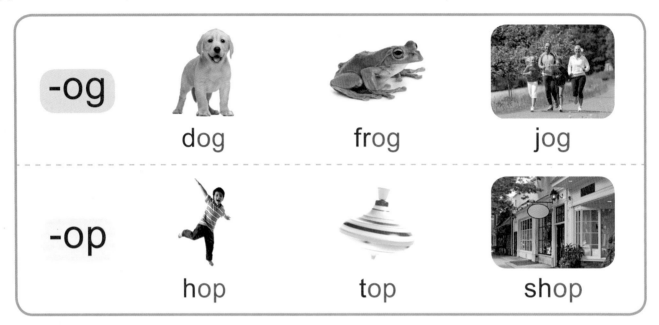

-og

dog   frog   jog

-op

hop   top   shop

B Listen, trace, and circle.

1. hop

2. dog

3. frog

4. shop

Listen, find, and write.

1.

og

og

fr

2.

op

op

sh

jog   shop   hop   dog   top   frog

D **Listen and write.**

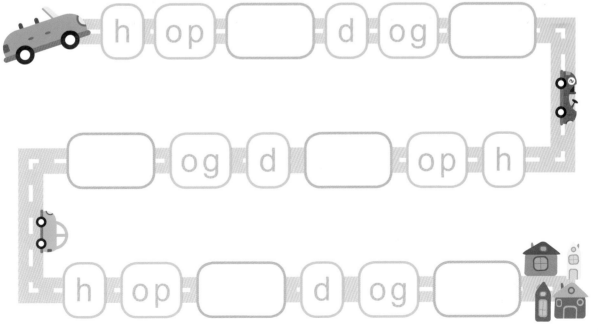

h | op | | d | og |

 | og | d | | op | h

h | op | | d | og |

E Look, circle, and write.

1.

fr_____

| og |
| ee |
| om |

2.
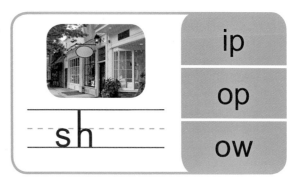

sh_____

| ip |
| op |
| ow |

3.
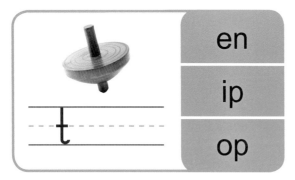

t_____

| en |
| ip |
| op |

4.
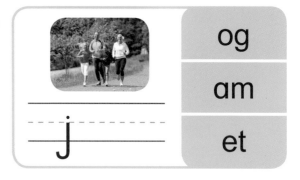

j_____

| og |
| am |
| et |

F Read and check.

1. It is a frog.

2. There is a shop.

3. It is a dog.

4. He is hopping.

G **Find and place the stickers.** stickers 1

1.

| d | |
| j | |

2.

| h | |
| t | |

H **Look, circle, and write.**

1.

frog   dog   top

F_____s are singing in the lake.

2.

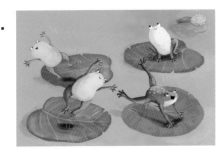

shop   hop   jog

They _____ from plant to plant.

2 Word Families -ock & -oss

A Listen and repeat.

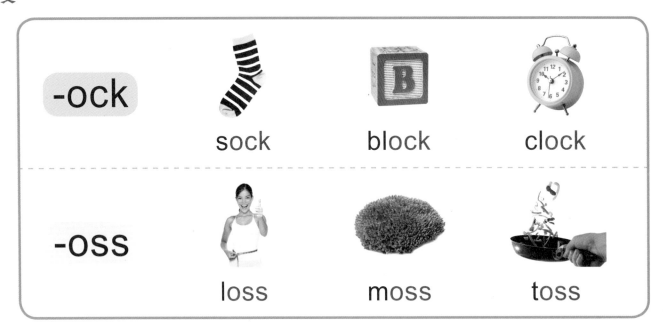

-ock

sock block clock

-oss

loss moss toss

B Listen and circle the ending letters.

1.

-ock   -oss

2.

-ock   -oss

3.

-ock   -oss

4.

-ock   -oss

5.

-ock   -oss

6.

-ock   -oss

C Listen and match.

1. cl •

ock

2. t •

3. m •

oss

4. bl •

D Listen, number, and write.

◯
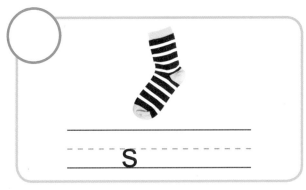
_____ s _____

◯

_____ m _____

◯
_____ bl _____

◯
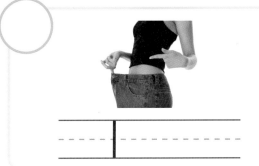
_____ l _____

E Look and write.

1.  bl + ____ → block

____ + ock → ____

2. ____ + ock → ____

s + ____ → sock

3.  ____ + oss → loss

l + ____ → ____

4. cl + ____ → ____

____ + ock → clock

F Look, read, and circle.

1.
toss
moss

2.
block
clock

3.
block
sock

4.
moss
loss

-ock

-oss

H **Look, circle, and write.**

1.

clock   sock   block

There is a big _____ tower.

2.

loss   moss   toss

You can see green _____ on the tower.

3 Word Families -ub & -ug

A Listen and repeat.

-ub

cub   rub   tub

-ug

bug   hug   mug

B Listen and circle the pictures with the same ending sounds.

1.

-ub

2.

-ug

C   Listen, circle, and write.

1. ![bear cub]
   -ub   -ug
   c ub

2. ![hug]
   -ub   -ug
   h

3. ![mug]
   -ub   -ug
   m

4. ![ladybug]
   -ub   -ug
   b

5. ![tub]
   -ub   -ug
   t

6. ![rub]
   -ub   -ug
   r

D   Listen, trace, and write.

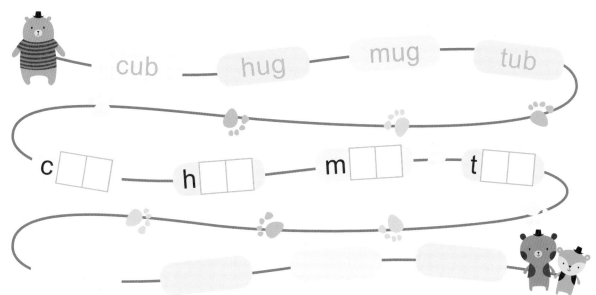

cub   hug   mug   tub

c☐☐   h☐☐   m☐☐   t☐☐

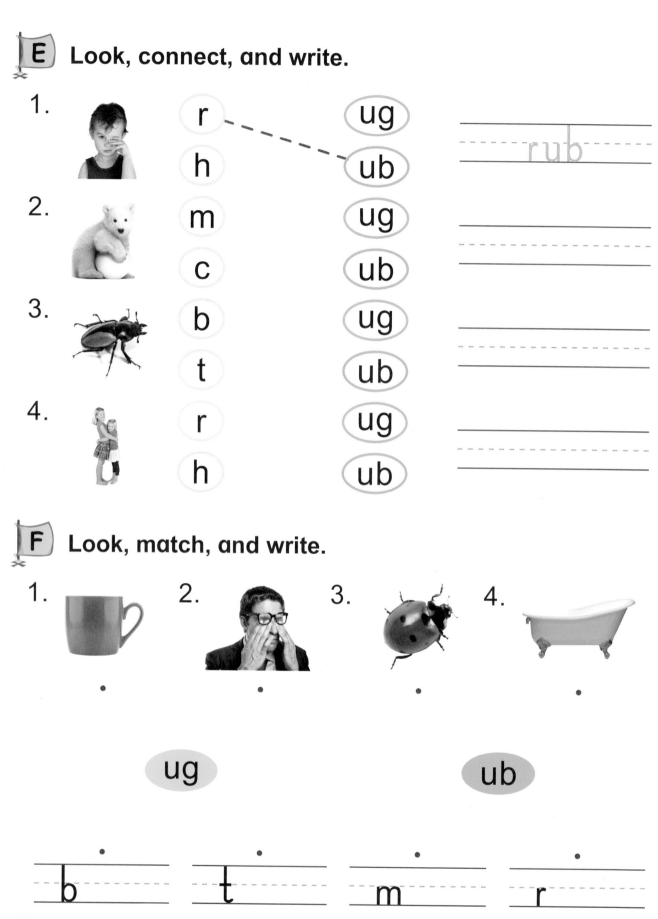

E Look, connect, and write.

1. r — ug
   ub
   h ... ub

   rub

2. m ug
   c ub

3. b ug
   t ub

4. r ug
   h ub

F Look, match, and write.

1.   2.   3.   4.

ug   ub

b   t   m   r

G Read and check.

1. It is a red mug.

2. It is a lion cub.

3. He likes to hug.

H Look, circle, and write.

1.

| mug | tub | cub |

A bear _____ is rubbing his nose on his mom.

2.

| hug | rub | bug |

Mom gives him a big _____ and a thousand kisses.

Unit 2 Andy's Birthday

- **Listen to the story.**
- **Listen and circle.**

It is Andy's birthday. Look at his **f**ace!
He looks very happy!

face

He gets a baseball bat for his birthday.
He swings!

Oops! He breaks Mom's favorite **v**ase.

vase

"Inside, you should play with your **tr**ain."

train

"You should **pl**a**y** baseball outside.
Don't play inside!" Mom says.
"Sorry, Mom! I will play outside!"

play

He checks the **m**a**i**l box.
There is a card from Grandma.

mail

"Happy birthday, Andy!" everybody says.

7

Everyone enjoys Andy's chocolate birthday **cake**.

8

cake

1 Long Vowel a: a_e

A Listen and repeat.

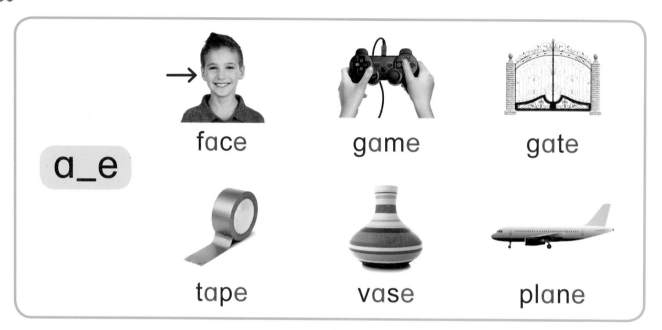

a_e

face   game   gate

tape   vase   plane

B Listen and number.

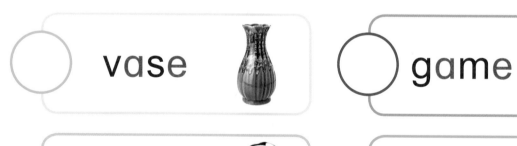

vase   game

face →   tape

gate   plane

C Listen, write, and match.

1. _____

   vase   •

2. _____

   - - - - - - - - - - •

   _____

3. _____

   - - - - - - - - - - •

   _____

4. _____

   - - - - - - - - - - •

   _____

D Listen and circle.

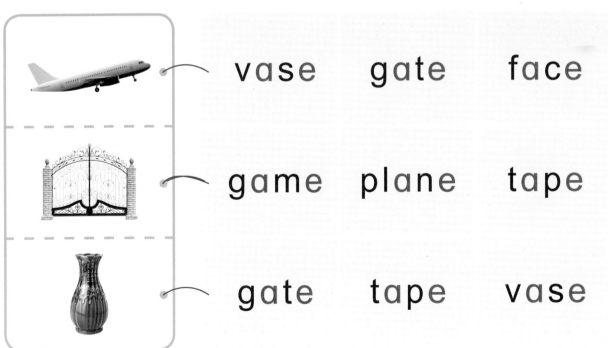

vase   gate   face

game   plane   tape

gate   tape   vase

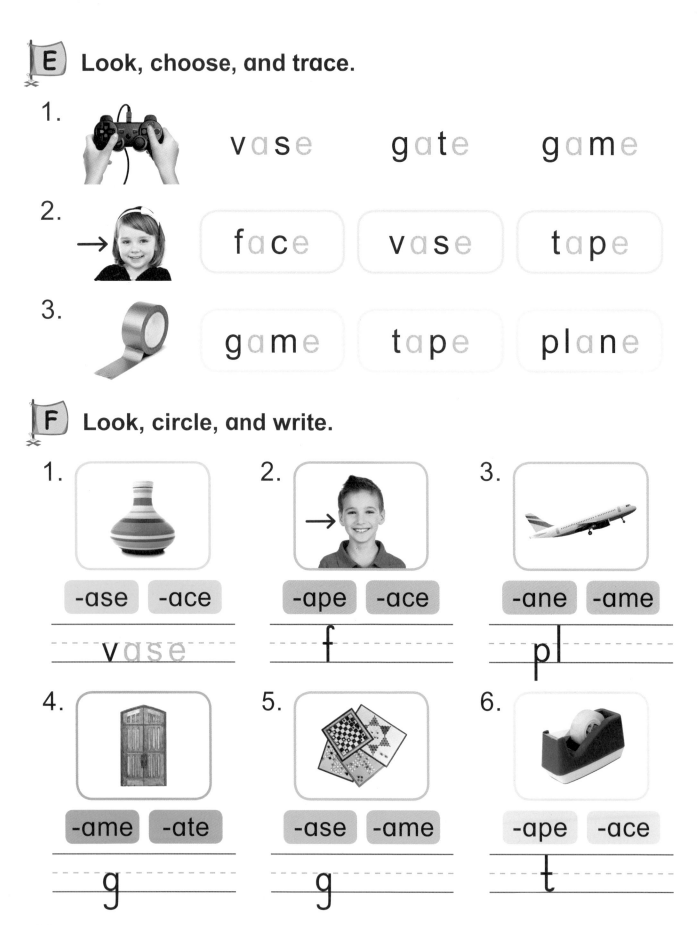

E Look, choose, and trace.

1. vase   gate   game

2. face   vase   tape

3. game   tape   plane

F Look, circle, and write.

1. -ase -ace   vase

2. -ape -ace   f

3. -ane -ame   pl

4. -ame -ate   g

5. -ase -ame   g

6. -ape -ace   t

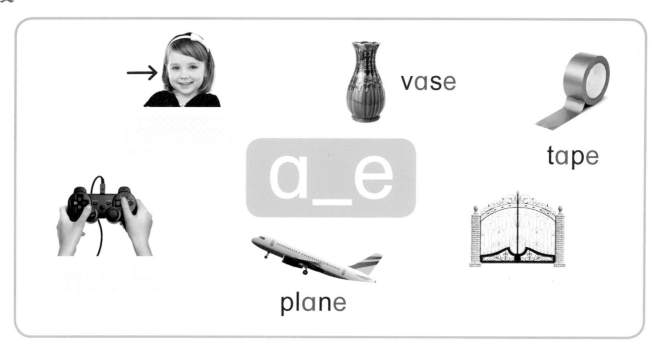

vase

tape

a_e

plane

H Look, circle, and write.

1.

game   plane   face

Look at his _____! He looks very happy!

2.

vase   tape   gate

Oops! He breaks Mom's favorite _____.

2 Long Vowel a: **ai** & **ay**

A Listen and repeat.

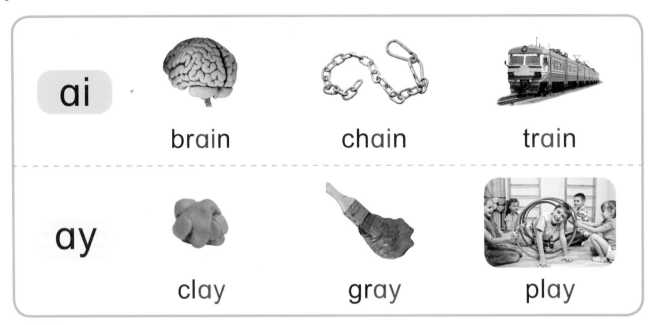

ai

brain   chain   train

ay

clay   gray   play

B Listen and trace.

1.

train

2.

brain

3.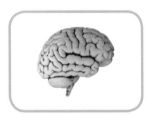

chain

4.

gray

5.

clay

6.

play

C Listen, trace, and circle.

1. **br**a**in**

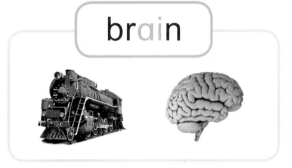

2. **pl**ay

3. **gr**ay

4. **ch**a**in**

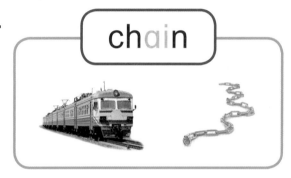

D Listen and write.

1.

		a	i	

2.

		a	i	

3.

		a	y

4.

		a	y

E Look, match, and trace.

1.

brain

play

2.

3.

chain

clay

4.

5.

train

gray

6.

F Look, read, and check.

1.

She plays with clay. ☐

She plays with a train. ☐

2.

He plays with a chain. ☐

He plays with a train. ☐

1.  clay

2. brain

3.  train

4. chain

5.  gray

6.  play

 H Look, circle, and write.

1.

brain   train   chain

You should play with your _____ .

2.

play   gray   clay

You should _____ baseball outside.

3 Word Families -ail & -ake

A Listen and repeat.

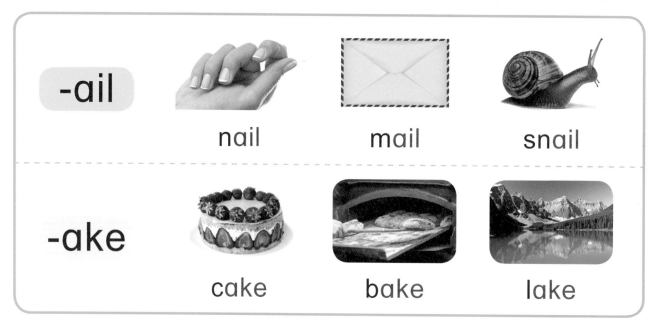

-ail

nail   mail   snail

-ake

cake   bake   lake

B Listen, number, and match.

◯ snail   ◯ bake   ◯ cake   ◯ mail

C Listen and circle the pictures with the same ending sounds.

1. mail

2. bake

D Listen, choose, and trace.

1. nail | mail

2. cake | lake

3. bake | cake

4. snail | mail

5. lake | bake

6. nail | snail

E Look, choose, and write.

1.

   -ail -ake

   lake

2. -ail -ake

   n____

3. -ail -ake

   c____

4. -ail -ake

   b____

5. -ail -ake

   sn____

6. -ail -ake

   m____

F Look, read, and circle.

1.  She checks a snail / mail .

2. 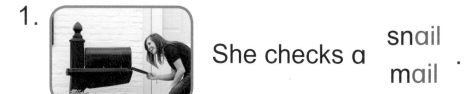 There is a cake / lake on the table.

3.  I like to lake / bake cookies.

G **Color the -ail words in pink and the -ake words in blue.**

	bake	**snail**
cake		**nail**
mail	**lake**	

H **Look, circle, and write.**

1.

mail   nail   snail

He checks the _____ box.

2.

lake   bake   cake

They enjoy Andy's chocolate birthday _____.

Summer Festival

■ **Listen to the story.**　　■ **Listen and circle.**

 T9

It is summer now.

1

You can feel the **heat**.

2

heat

Bees buzz around a hive.

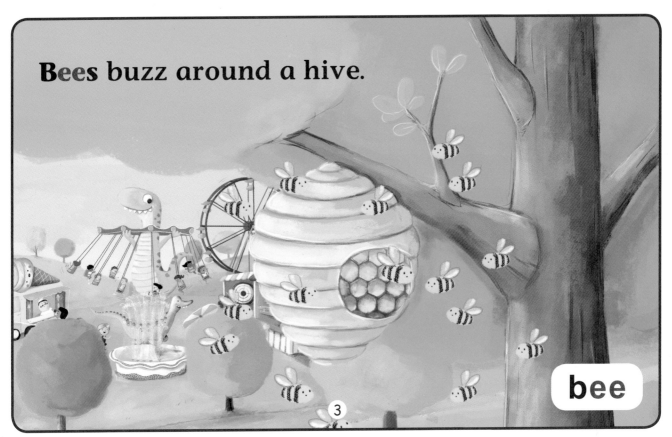

bee

3

A boy rides a **bike**.

bike

4

Delicious **pies lie** on the table.

pie

A puppy **sleeps** under a tree.

sleep

Girls play with dice.

7

dice

Everyone has fun at the festival.

8

1 Long Vowel e: **ea** & **ee**

A Listen and repeat.

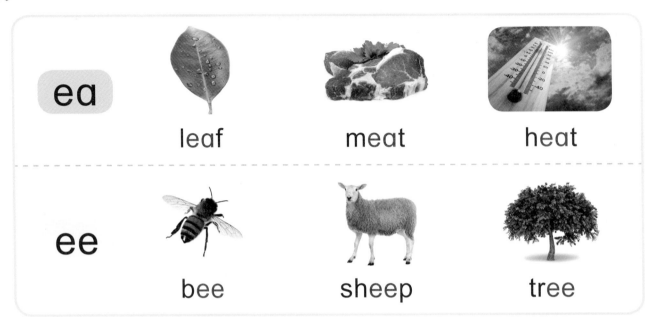

ea

leaf   meat   heat

ee

bee   sheep   tree

B Listen, circle, and write.

1. sheep

2. heat

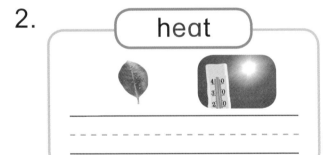

3. bee

4. meat

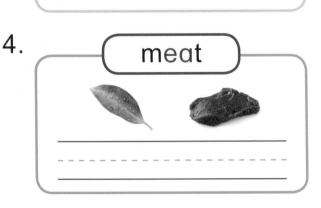

C Listen, find, and write.

1.

ea

_____   _____   _____

- -

_____   _____   _____

2.

ee

_____   _____   _____

- -

_____   _____   _____

| tree   leaf   heat   bee   sheep   meat |

D Listen, match, and trace.

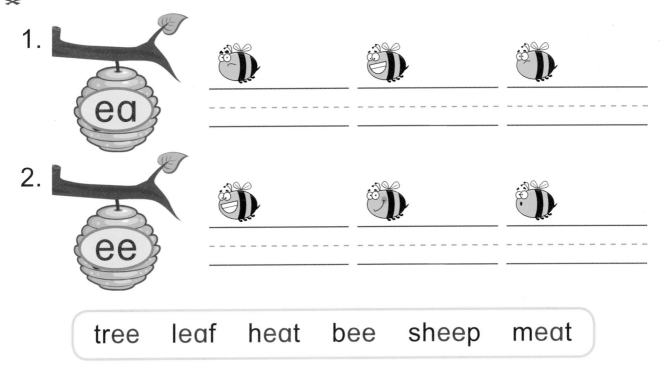

1.
•
• leaf

ea

2.
•
• bee

3.
•
• meat

ee

4.
•
• tree

Look and write.

1.
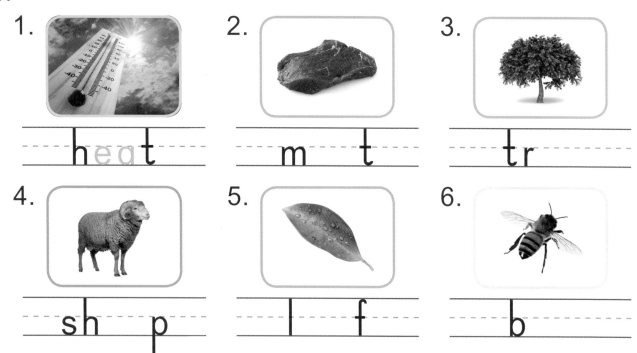

h e a t

2.

m ___ t

3.

tr ___ ___

4.

sh ___ p

5.

l ___ ___ f

6.

b ___ ___

F **Find and write.**

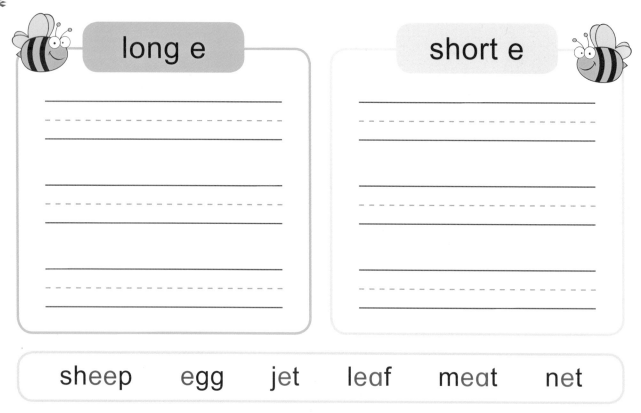

long e	short e

sheep   egg   jet   leaf   meat   net

G **Find and place the stickers.** stickers 1

1.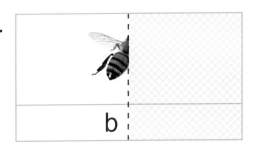
b

2.
sh

3.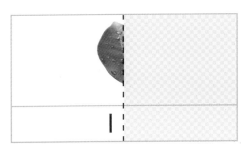
l

4.
tr

H **Look, circle, and write.**

1.

meat   leaf   heat

You can feel the _____.

2.

sheep   bee   tree

B_____s buzz around a hive.

2 Long Vowel i: **i_e** & **ie**

A Listen and repeat.

i_e	bike	five	smile
ie	pie	tie	lie

B Listen and trace.

1. pie
2. tie
3. lie
4. five
5. bike
6. smile

C Listen and circle.

1.

five   bike

2.

lie   tie

3.

bike   pie

4.

smile   five

D Listen and color.    long i   short i

igloo	five	bike
lie	milk	ink
wig	tie	smile

E Look, write, and match.

1.

sm __ l

2.

b __ k

i_e

3.

__ t

4.

p __

ie

5.

f __ v

6.

__ l

F Read and circle.

1.

i_e   There are (five) bikes on the street.

2.

ie   Dad is wearing a tie and eating pies.

G Read and check.

1.

I have a red bike.

2.

It is number five.

3.

They lie on the grass.

H Look, circle, and write.

1.

five   bike   lie

A boy rides a _____.

2.

pie   tie   smile

Delicious _____s lie on the table.

3 Word Families -eep & -ice

A Listen and repeat.

-eep

jeep sheep sleep

-ice

dice mice rice

B Listen and circle the ending letters.

1.

-eep -ice

2.

-eep -ice

3.

-eep -ice

4.

-eep -ice

5.

-eep -ice

6.

-eep -ice

 C **Listen and write.**

1.

r +

_____
- - - - - - - - - - - -
_____

2.

j +

_____
- - - - - - - - - - - -
_____

3.

sh +

_____
- - - - - - - - - - - -
_____

4.

d +

_____
- - - - - - - - - - - -
_____

 D **Listen, trace, and write.**

 dice →  mice →  rice →  jeep

 j → 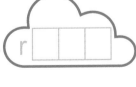 r ← 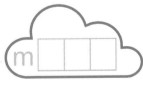 m ←  d

 →  →  →

E Look, connect, and write.

1. 
   (r)   (eep)
   (j)   (ice)   _rice_

2. 
   (m)   (eep)
   (d)   (ice)   _____

3. 
   (m)   (eep)
   (sh)   (ice)   _____

4. 
   (sl)   (eep)
   (d)   (ice)   _____

F Look, read, and circle.

1. 
   sheep
   sleep

2. 
   dice
   rice

3. 
   jeep
   sheep

4. 
   mice
   rice

G Find and place the stickers. stickers 2

1.

sh	
sl	

2.

r	
d	

H Look, circle, and write.

1.

sleep   sheep   jeep

A puppy _____s under a tree.

2.

rice   dice   mice

Girls play with _____.

Lunch at School

■ Listen to the story. ■ Listen and circle. T13

The bell rings! It is lunch time.
Everyone goes to the cafeteria.

Cafeteria

1

Brian is having **toast** with jam.

toast

2

There is **a rose** on the table.

rose

Don't be **rude** at the table.

rude

The **school** cafeteria is full of children.

⑤

Sally is wearing a **blue** dress.

6

blue

Sally has her lunch in a **brown** bag.

⑦

brown

The bell rings again.
It is time to go back to class!

8

1 Long Vowel o: oa & o_e

A Listen and repeat.

| oa | boat | goat | toast |
| o_e | note | nose | rose |

B Listen and number.

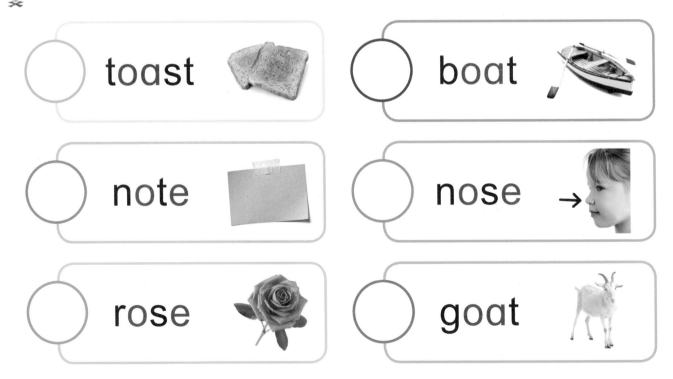

○ toast

○ boat

○ note

○ nose

○ rose

○ goat

C Listen and circle.

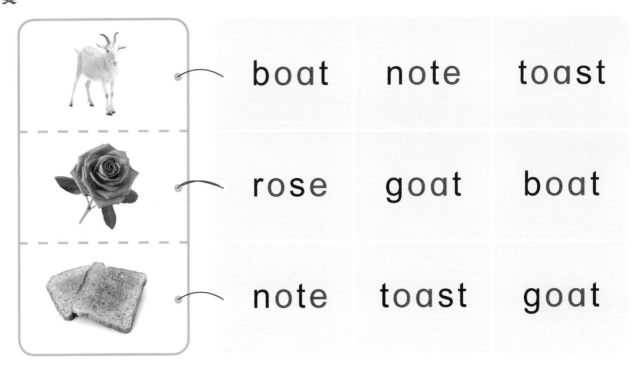

boat	note	toast
rose	goat	boat
note	toast	goat

 D Listen, circle, and write.

1.

2.

3.

4.

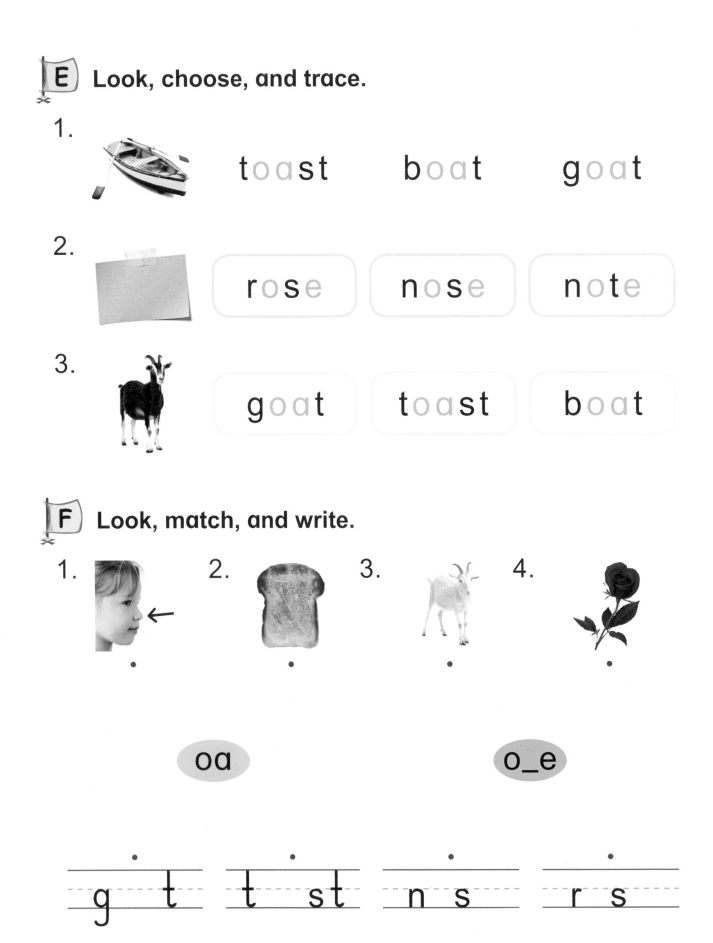

E Look, choose, and trace.

1. toast   boat   goat

2. rose   nose   note

3. goat   toast   boat

F Look, match, and write.

1.   2.   3.   4.

oa   o_e

g t   t st   n s   r s

G Find and write.

long o	short o
_____	_____
_____	_____
_____	_____
_____	_____

rose   goat   olive   pot   boat   log

H Look, circle, and write.

1.

goat   toast   boat

_____

Brian is having _____ with jam.

2.

nose   rose   note

_____

There is a _____ on the table.

② Long Vowel u: **u_e** & **oo**

A Listen and repeat.

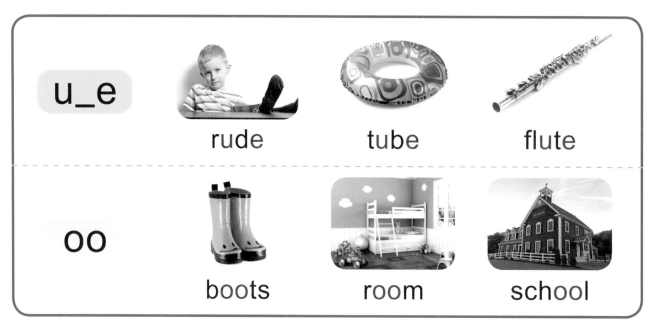

u_e	rude	tube	flute
oo	boots	room	school

B Listen, number, and match.

◯ room　◯ rude　◯ school　◯ boots

C Listen, choose, and trace.

1. rude | tube

2. room | boots

3. school | room

4. flute | rude

5. tube | flute

6. boots | school

D Listen and circle the words with the long u sound.

1. school   umbrella   jump

2. hungry   rude   under

3. umbrella   run   tube

4. flute   hungry   up

E Look, circle, and write.

1.
u_e   **oo**

sch**oo**l

2.
u_e   **oo**

r _ _ m

3.
u_e   oo

_ r _ d

4.
u_e   oo

fl _ t

5.
u_e   **oo**

b _ _ ts

6.
u_e   oo

t _ b _

F Read and check.

1.
I have yellow
boots.

2.
It is a swimming
tube.

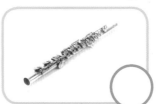

3.
I like to go to
school.

G Find and place the stickers. stickers 1

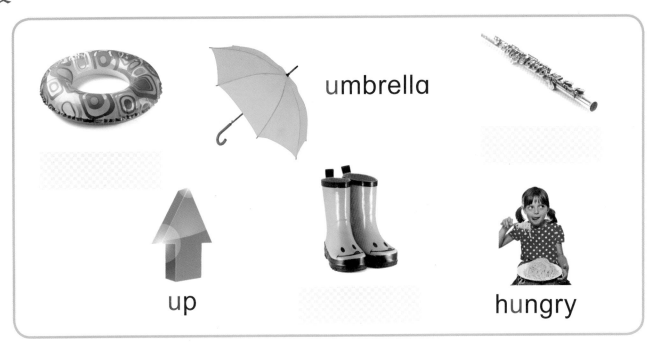

umbrella

up

hungry

H Look, circle, and write.

1.

tube   flute   rude

Don't be _____ at the table.

2.

school   room   boots

The _____ cafeteria is full of children.

3 Word Families -own & -ue

A Listen and repeat.

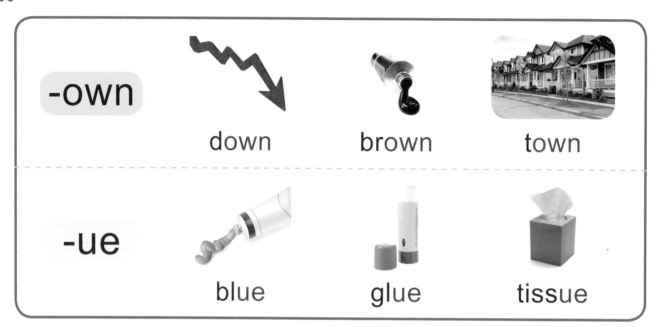

-own

down   brown   town

-ue

blue   glue   tissue

B Listen and circle the ending letters.

1.

-own -ue

2.

-own -ue

3.

-own -ue

4.

-own -ue

5.

-own -ue

6.

-own -ue

C Listen, trace, and write.

1. **t**own

2. **bl**ue

3. **br**own

4. **gl**ue

D Listen, number, and write.

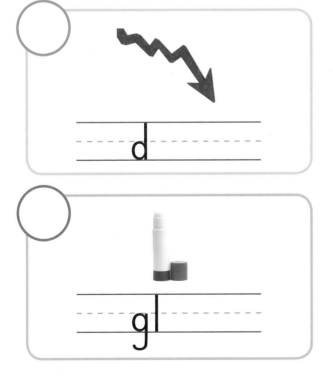

○ d

○ br

○ gl

○ bl

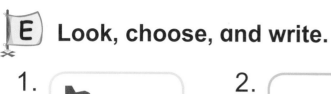

E Look, choose, and write.

1.

-own · -ue

d own

2.

-own · -ue

br

3.

-own · -ue

bl

4.

-own · -ue

tiss

5.

-own · -ue

gl

6.

-own · -ue

t

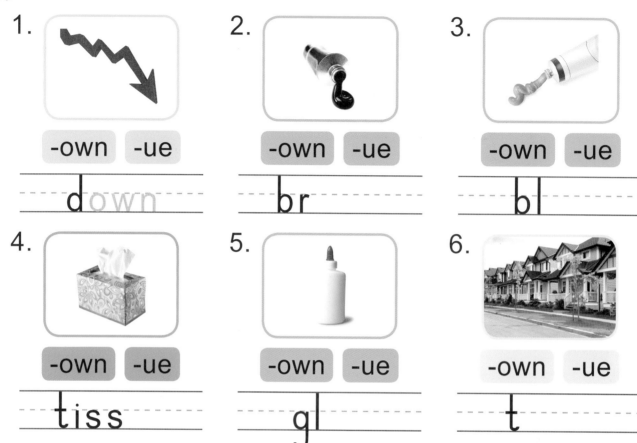

F Look, read, and circle.

1.

town

down

2.

tissue

glue

3.

glue

blue

4.

down

brown

G Find and place the stickers.

-own

-ue

H Look, circle, and write.

1.

blue   glue   tissue

Sally is wearing a _____ dress.

2.

town   brown   down

Sally has her lunch in a _____ bag.

Phonics Song

⭐ **Sing a song.**

Keep the rhythm with me!

A I ai ai	brain chain train
A Y ay ay	clay play gray
A I L ail ail	mail nail snail
A K E ake ake	bake cake lake
E A ea ea	heat meat leaf
E E ee ee	bee tree sheep
E E P eep eep	jeep sheep sleep
I C E ice ice	dice mice rice
O A oa oa	boat goat toast
O O oo oo	boot room school
O W N own own	down town brown
U E ue ue	blue glue tissue

Wow! Look at all the words we read!

Answer Key 1

Unit 1 Spring Has Come!

p. 2~5

frog hop cub

hug clock moss

p. 6

B 1. hop, 2. dog,

3. frog, 4. shop,

p. 7

C 1. dog, jog, frog

2. top, hop, shop

D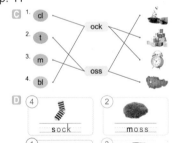

p. 8

E 1. og, frog 2. op, shop

3. op, top 4. og, jog

F 1. 2. 3. 4.

p. 9

G 1. og 2. op

H 1. Frog 2. hop

p. 10

B 1. -ock 2. -ock 3. -oss

4. -oss 5. -ock 6. -oss

p. 11

C 1. cl 2. t 3. m 4. bl

ock oss

D 4. sock 2. moss 1. block 3. loss

p. 12

E 1. bl+ock → block

2. s+ock → sock

3. l+oss → loss

4. cl+ock → clock

F 1. toss 2. clock

3. sock 4. moss

p. 13

G -ock. -oss.

H 1. clock 2. moss

p. 14

B 1. 2.

p. 15

C 1. -ub, cub 2. -ug, hug

3. -ug, mug 4. -ug, bug

5. -ub, tub 6. -ub, rub

D

cub — hug — mug — tub

c u b — h u g — m u g — tub

cub — hug — mug — tub

p. 16

E 1. r-ub, rub 2. c-ub, cub

3. b-ug, bug 4. h-ug, hug

F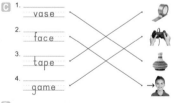

ug ub

bug tub mug rub

p. 17

G 1. 2. 3.

H 1. cub 2. hug

Unit 2 Andy's Birthday

p. 18~21

face vase train

play mail cake

p. 22

B 2 → 5 → 3 → 1 → 6 → 4

p. 23

C 1. vase 2. face 3. tape 4. game

D vase gate face

game plane tape

gate tape vase

p. 24

E 1. game 2. face 3. tape

F 1. -ase, vase 2. -ace, face

3. -ane, plane 4. -ate, gate

5. -ame, game 6. -ape, tape

p. 25

G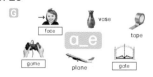

face vase tape

a_e game plane gate

H 1. face 2. vase

p. 26

B 1. train 2. brain 3. chain

4. gray 5. clay 6. play

p. 27

C 1. brain, 2. play,

3. gray, 4. chain,

D 1. train 2. brain 3. clay 4. gray

p. 28

E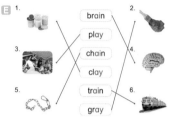
1. brain play chain clay train gray

F 1. She plays with clay.

2. He plays with a train.

p. 29

G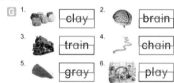
1. clay 2. brain 3. train 4. chain 5. gray 6. play

H 1. train 2. play

p. 30

B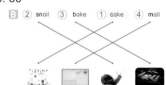
2 snail 3 bake 1 cake 4 mail

p. 31

C 1. 2.

D 1. nail 2. lake 3. cake

4. mail 5. bake 6. snail

p. 32

E 1. -ake, lake 2. -ail, nail

3. -ake, cake 4. -ake, bake

5. -ail, snail 6. -ail, mail

F 1. mail 2. cake 3. bake

p. 33

G
bake snail cake nail mail lake

H 1. mail 2. cake

67

Unit 3 Summer Festival

p. 34~37

heat  bee bike

pie sleep dice

p. 38

B 1. 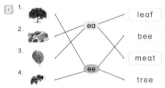 sheep   2. heat

3. bee   4. meat

p. 39

C 1. leaf, meat, heat

2. tree, sheep, bee

D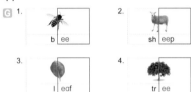
1. — ea — leaf
2. — — bee
3. — ee — meat
4. — — tree

p. 40

E 1. heat   2. meat   3. tree
4. sheep   5. leaf   6. bee

F long e: sheep, leaf, meat
short e: egg, jet, net

p. 41

G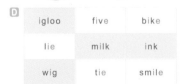
1. b | ee   2. sh | eep
3. l | eaf   4. tr | ee

H 1. heat 2. Bee

p. 42

B 1. pie   2. tie   3. lie
4. five   5. bike   6. smile

p. 43

C 1. bike 2. lie

3. pie 4. five

D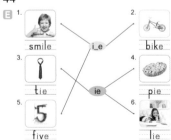

igloo	five	bike
lie	milk	ink
wig	tie	smile

p. 44

E
1. smile — i_e — bike
3. tie — — 4. pie
2. — ie — 6.
5. five — — lie

F 1. i_e There are (five) (bikes) on the street.

2. ie Dad is wearing a (tie) and eating (pies)

p. 45

G 1.  2. 3.

H 1. bike 2. pie

p. 46

B 1. -ice   2. -ice   3. -eep
4. -ice   5. -eep   6. -eep

p. 47

C 1. r+ice, rice
2. j+eep, jeep
3. sh+eep, sheep
4. d+ice, dice

D
dice | mice | rice | jeep
jeep | rice | mice | dice
dice | mice | rice | jeep

p. 48

E 1. r-ice, rice   2. d-ice, dice
3. m-ice, mice   4. sl-eep, sleep

F 1. sleep 2. dice 3. jeep 4. mice

p. 49

G 1. eep 2. ice

H 1. sleep 2. dice

Unit 4 Lunch at School

p. 50~53

toast  rose rude

blue brown

p. 54

B 5 → 3 → 4 → 1 → 2 → 6

p. 55

C
boat note (toast)
(rose) (goat) boat
note (toast) (goat)

D 1. boat   2. nose

3. note   4. toast

p. 56

E 1. boat 2. note 3. goat

F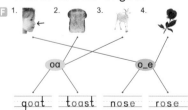
1. ← 2. 3. 4.
— oa — o_e —
goat toast nose rose

p. 57

G long o: rose, boat, goat
short o: log, olive, pot

H 1. toast 2. rose

p. 58

B 2 room 3 rude 4 school 1 boots
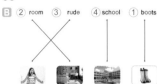

p. 59

C 1. tube   2. room   3. school
4. rude   5. flute   6. boots

D 1. school   2. rude
3. tube   4. flute

p. 60

E 1. oo, school   2. oo, room
3. u_e, rude   4. u_e, flute
5. oo, boots   6. u_e, tube

F 1.   2.   3.

G
tube   umbrella   flute
up   boots   hungry

H 1. rude 2. school

p. 62

B 1. -own   2. -ue   3. -own
4. -ue   5. -ue   6. -own

p. 63

C 1. town,   2. blue,
3. brown,   4. glue,

D
1 down   4 brown
3 glue   2 blue

p. 64

E 1. -own, down   2. -own, brown
3. -ue, blue   4. -ue, tissue
5. -ue, glue   6. -own, town

F 1. down   2. tissue
3. blue   4. brown

p. 65

G -own.   -ue.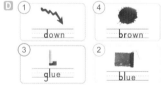

H 1. blue 2. brown

stickers 1

op   og

stickers 1

face   gate

game

stickers 2

clay   chain

gray   train

brain   play

stickers 1

ee   ee

eep   eaf

stickers 2

ice   eep

stickers 2

stickers 1

tube   boots   flute